31 DAY
DEVO...

Among the Butterflies

KARLA ELDER

ARROW PRESS

Copyright © 2024 Karla Elder

All rights reserved. No part of this publication may be reproduced, distributed, or transmitted in any form or by any means, including photocopying, recording, or other electronic or mechanical methods, without the prior written permission of the publisher, except in the case of brief quotations embodied in critical reviews and certain other noncommercial uses permitted by copyright law. For permission requests, write to the publisher, addressed "Attention: Permissions Coordinator," at the address below.

Paperback: 978-1-951475-31-4
Ebook: 978-1-951475-32-1

Library of Congress Control Number: 2024904811

First paperback edition: May 2024

Any references to historical events, real people, or real places are used fictitiously. Names, characters, and places are products of the author's imagination.

Edited by Avodah Editorial Services
Cover Art by Amanda Blake Designs
Layout by Amanda Blake Designs

Arrow Press Publishing
Summerville, SC 29486

www.arrowpresspublishing.com

Contents

SECTION 1 · · · · · · · · · · · · · · · · 6
THE BEGINNING

SECTION 2 · · · · · · · · · · · · · · · · 44
THE CATERPILLAR

SECTION 3 · · · · · · · · · · · · · · · · 82
THE CHRYSALIS

SECTION 4 · · · · · · · · · · · · · · · · 112
THE BUTTERFLY

Introduction

God chose you before you chose this book. Are you seeking change in your life? Tired of the mediocrity of your days? Do you wonder if there is more to your days than what you are tapping in to? A breakthrough is needed but how do you get there? Learning to lean into and wait on God as you push through demands for you to remain steadfast in your heart. Romans 5:3-5 teaches you that suffering produces endurance, and endurance produces character and character produces hope, and hope does not put us to shame, because God's love has been poured into our hearts through the Holy Spirit who has been given to us. This book gives you the tools to meet you right where you are. It is broken down into the four life cycles of the butterfly. Understanding and applying God's knowledge will bring you forth into His wisdom actively moving in your life. Each cycle brings you through the shedding away of self and leaning into the next season reflecting the guidance of God's direction as His divine metamorphosis takes place over your life. Your story of transformation is meant to be shared with others to encourage them along their journey. This 31 day devotion is meant to be viewed as 31 divine appointments of your journey of hope. Stay on each day as long as needed until you feel led to move to the next day. There is a place to reflect and take notes following each divine appointment. Be encouraged as you press into your breakthrough and move through the metamorphosis into God's calling over your life as you soar with wings of hope.

SECTION 1

THE BEGINNING
is for such a time as this

PSALM 32:8

You have been chosen to be in this exact moment in time. You are perfectly made with a unique calling unto His purpose over all the days of your life. Don't be afraid to step into this new territory in which you are discovering the new you. You are safely growing into the promises of God as you feed on His word. God is changing you from the inside out. Your heart is postured in peace as you leave behind the things of old and embrace the things of new. God's sovereign hand is always near guiding you through His fresh mercies and grace with each day. Daily delight in God as you meet with Him in prayer. He waits to hear from you as you enter His gates with thanksgiving and petitioning your request throughout your day. Claim the promises of wisdom as you apply truth to sin and resist temptation. Rest under His Almighty hand. Remain vigilant and sober to the lies and schemes of the devil. You are richly blessed and highly favored by the promises of God spoken over you. His breath is in your lungs. Breath in hope as you were made for such a time as this.

DAY 1

CREATE ROOM

And he said unto me, My grace is sufficient for thee: for my strength is made perfect in weakness. Most gladly, therefore, will I rather glory in my infirmities that the power of Christ may rest upon me. Therefore, I take pleasure in infirmities, in reproaches, in necessities, in persecutions, in distresses for Christ's sake: for when I am weak, then am I strong.

2 CORINTHIANS 12:9-10 (KJV)

God is waiting for you to make room for Him in your life. Will you pencil Him in, just in case you need to reschedule? Or will you set His time in ink, representing time set aside without change? God is waiting and is nearest in your moments of brokenness and weakness. It's in your yes to surrender that His yes merges to give you strength as He carries you through.

When you are at your most vulnerable place and you surrender, God hears your surrender as a yes. He then meets you and intersects your yes with His yes. His yes will deliver you from a place of despair to a place of fresh hope. A place where new opportunities will display His power in your life.

Take a moment before reading God's word to meet him in prayer to posture your heart and mind to be still in His presence. It is here that you will feel the shift from helplessness to hopefulness. You will be clothed in good courage as you get focused on what He is saying to you. He is both leading and grooming you. He also is going before you and making a way for you to journey into new territory. Boldly take your first step into His plan for you.

Oh, how He loves you! His plans for you are beyond your deepest comprehension and your furthest expectations. He has chosen you for this time and season. You are clothed in peace beyond understanding. Your soul rests in the knowledge gained and wisdom granted to walk in boldness. You have the mind of Christ. Now, walk boldly in His promises to prosper and not harm you. His provision is His song of love over you.

CREATE ROOM 1

Where do you see God's grace being sufficient over your life?

DAY 2: DON'T MISS IT!

> *The book of the law shall not depart out of thy mouth; but thou shalt meditate therein day and night, that thou mayest observe to do according to all that is written therein: for then thou shalt make thy way prosperous, and then thou shalt have good success.*

JOSHUA 1:8 (KJV)

Are you ready? Are you anticipating what God has for you? Right now, in this very moment before you take one more step into mediocrity; make a shift. Posture your heart in prayer and praise with bellows of thanksgiving. God's love towards you flows freely with promises of restoration into newness. He is a good father. Leave your grave clothes worn by the old man behind and put on your garments of praise in the newness of you. Look and see what great things God has done! You are going in a new direction with a new vision. No need for things of the past to remind you of where you've been. Press on to the good mark that lies ahead.

There are rivers of flowing living water waiting to be given to all who thirst. Don't miss an opportunity each day to share His hope with the world around you. His love endures forever. Tell your story and watch God move throughout it. Embracing His presence is the best gift to pass along. Don't doubt yourself, you were made for such a time as this. He has called you to it and has completely given you all that is needed to complete it.

Don't try to figure out your way to do it; just reach out and take the hand of Jesus. He will lead you. Partner with the Holy Spirit as you lean into his guidance. May you see your value through God's eyes as you boldly step into the tasks before you.. You are called, chosen and loved with an expectancy of excellence. God spoke your calling into your life before He covered you in your Mother's womb. Don't miss this!

God has the first and last word over your life. His words are your solid foundation. Building on any other foundation will not stand the storms of time. God's word has no loopholes or fine print throughout your seasons of change. He has a perfect plan for your life. He sees your tears in the battles of your life. He will fight for you. He will comfort you and encourage you when your soul aches and only groans can be heard by God. Rejoice in knowing that He has the last word, the unchanging Word of God wrapped in His unending love.

DON'T MISS IT! 2

What did you shift in your life to align with God?

DAY 3
CHOSEN, NOT FORSAKEN

And they that know thy name will put their trust in thee: for thou, Lord, has not forsaken them that seek thee. Sing praises to the Lord which dwelleth in Zion: declare among the people his doings.

PSALM 9:10-11 (KJV)

You may be in the wilderness, but this is not your place of residence. This, too, is for but a season. You are chosen to live in the land of milk and honey. Going through the wilderness is necessary to get to the abundant life God has called you into.

Although you may feel like you are walking about on barren land, God is your provider. The growth in this season is from the sparse plant life you will encounter. The growth is from within as you lean and learn on God in a way like never before. This is not a land of punishment but of preparation of God's divine plan for your chosen life. His faithfulness is a true treasure never more valued than when it is all you must cling to. Even when you are walking through what may seem like a barren land, God is bringing forth a new thing. Rejoice and be glad in it as He reveals His new purpose in your life.

Speak God's Word over your life. Confidently speak His promises over all that you minister to in both your words and deed. The gift of God's word is meant to be passed on. Just like in prayer it is essential to the change and rebuilding of your character to reflect God's character. God is not about the quick fix, but the steady growth that takes root and bears good fruit. As you daily meditate upon His word accept the challenge to be renewed in His truth. Speak, declare and hold fast to the promises of God over your life. May you choose to remain steadfast as you hunger & thirst for His word. Embrace this fresh canvas of your life as you allow the light of God to shine through all your brokenness. Your life may reflect that of sharp and jagged pieces of glass but with God's love it will create a beautiful piece of art as in a stained-glass window when hope shines through it and its beauty resonates the presence of the Master.

Unmerited grace and mercy were freely given unto you but was bought with a high price of an everlasting love towards you when you were still a sinner. He hears your soul's groans and sees every tear. Your help comes from the one who watches over you. He will keep you from all trouble. His grace is sufficient unto all things. He promises that you will continue to grow in assurance and confidence daily as you lean into Jesus. He is near, take His hand. Walk alongside him and you will grow in wisdom as you become more aware of the choices you make and the lessons you apply to make better choices. The "New" you is struggling to come forth into this unknown territory where you recognize nothing but the presence of God. Beloved, you are chosen, redeemed and forgiven. You are moving in the direction that He has called you to journey through. Daily seek God in obedience out of your dependence on Him. Surrender in His wisdom as you grow in His wisdom and unique ways. May His goodness and grace abound with you all the days of your life. You are a sweet delight to Him always.

CHOSEN, NOT FORSAKEN 3

Where do you see the evidence of God in your progress?

DAY 4
NO AND NOT YET

The secret things belong unto the LORD our God: but those things which are revealed belong unto us and to our children for ever, that we may do all the words of this law.

DETERONOMY 29:29 (KJV)

God answers our prayers in one of three ways; yes, no, or not yet. As an adult, you too have handed out these answers—to friends or colleagues, or possibly as a parent. Nonetheless, the latter two answers are often not so well received or accepted without an argument or grumbling and complaining at the least. As the one giving the answer, you quickly learn that you will not be seated in the chair of popularity often. Truth be told, you will see your fair share of disappointment on others' faces more than you care to. Inside of you is the core to your decision-making.

Love naturally builds a boundary to protect what/who is inside while keeping what's not safe on the outside of the boundary. God's love is your boundary. God can at times seem like a mystery. You can't know all His ways, but your trust is in Him alone. You can rest in confidence, knowing that He has your best interests at heart. Know this, all of His answers are for your best, and not any less. The secret things of God are revealed to you in due season.

His answers of "yes," "no," and "not yet" are never given without His love and provision attached. Remain in His boundaries where He has placed you to grow strong. Remain postured with a grateful heart as He reveals those things He has for you to pass on throughout generations.

As you embrace this day, commit to unite with your Heavenly Father. Approach His throne of grace and mercy, and let your first words be those unto Him with a heart posture in gratitude and joy. Don't stop the conversation; continue talking as He walks alongside you throughout this day. Today is a gift, also known as the present. Tomorrow is not promised. Be committed to daily talking before daily walking.

Talk to God first before you read His Word, as He loves to enlighten you with His wisdom. He treasures you and your time spent together. Seek Him in prayer and tell Him of your appreciation for all He has done and continues to do even in the most secret places of your life. Give gratitude before listing your needs. Surrender your life unto His will and walk boldly in obedience as He deepens your trust and belief in Him. As the one giving the answer, you quickly learn that you will not be seated in the chair of popularity often. Truth be told, you will see your fair share of disappointment on others' faces more than you care to. Inside of you is the core to your decision-making. You will find rest in His glorious hope. Pray first and forevermore.

NO AND NOT YET **4**

What things has God shown you in secret that belong to you?

DAY 5
WHAT'S CROWDING OUT YOUR PEACE?

But when the Comforter is come, whom I will send unto you from the Father, even the Spirit of truth, which proceedeth from the Father, he shall testify of me.

JOHN 15:26 (KJV)

What is robbing you of peace in your day? What caused your peace to be shifted? Peace is such a wonderful gift from above. Posture yourself to regain the space for peace again. How far will you go to find peace? Peace is not a physical location but a spiritual gift to be held as a priceless treasure. Still knowing this doesn't make you any more at peace. Contentment bears the fruit of peace. True contentment comes from having a relationship with the trinity; The Father, Son and Holy Spirit. The three in one is where your future lies. Having a relationship with each one of them brings different levels of the abundant life that God has chosen you to embrace. Just like any other person in your life, spending time with them is essential to learn of their character. While you are learning about each part of the trinity you are growing more into your calling through growing in wisdom and stature.

One way to grow in stature is by growing in wisdom. Gaining knowledge first comes before wisdom. Your obedience to be hungry and search after truth comes from a seed God placed in you from before birth. Where do you gain your knowledge? What fills your heart up with fulfillment? What are your priorities and how did you choose them? Truly we reflect what our family has modeled throughout our childhood. Some of these answers are things passed down through family.

Today is a new day, full of new opportunities to embark upon a road not yet travelled. Choose this day to grow in ways that you have never seen before you. Choose to grow deeper into the person God has called you to become. Look at the tools he has placed for you to grow through into a space so significant for just you. A place where he calls you, his child, to come and let His light shine through you.

Growing in your relationship with God does bring you to a place to surrender the worldly desires and mindsets. This is the place where mercy and grace are in every breath you breathe. It is where peace abounds with the Father, Son and Holy Spirit. This is the where transformation begins as your priorities are shaped through fasting and meditating on God's Word , where your knowledge turns to wisdom by the renewing of your mind. You now have the mind of Christ where your peace no longer will be crowded out.

WHAT'S CROWDING OUT YOUR PEACE? 5

How have you made peace a priority?

DAY 6
BE STILL AND JUST BE HELD

Fear thou not; for I am with thee: be not dismayed; for I am thy God: I will strengthen thee; I will help thee; yea, I will uphold thee with the right hand of my righteousness.

ISAIAH 41:10 (KJV)

Do you feel heavily burdened? Is worry keeping you from the rest that you desperately need? Worry is self-produced by thinking that you can solve your own problems without the intervention of a mighty all-knowing God. Why do you continue to stay chained to worry?

Search and grasp the truth you have placed behind your feelings. Know that when it appears that life is falling apart; it is often falling into place.

The areas of sin in your life bear the thorns of shame in your side. Rise up! Despite the thorn, stand firm in the posture of truth. God will reveal all issues that you need to cast upon Him to carry no more. As you cast your cares upon Him; He generously pours out His grace & mercy over your life. His love is a banner over your life. Being honest often brings you to a place of vulnerability. God meets you there with open arms and accepts you just as you are. Don't delay!

He will break your chains and help you to cast your cares on Him as you mature. You are walking with Him. He is your ever-present help to intercede on your part so that what once bound you will no longer influence you. Choose to be a vessel of joy and peace. You are no longer defined by the shame and hidden secrets of your past. Your weariness has been replaced by grace unending. Ask the Lord to search your heart and renew the areas that need to be surrendered unto Him.

Rest is vital to you in many areas of your life. You need physical rest as you overexert yourself in exercise in your daily life. You need rest at the end of your day for both mental and physical rest needed to move throughout your responsibilities. You also need spiritual rest. Come and rest in the shadow of the Almighty. He awaits for you to be still and be held.

BE STILL AND JUST BE HELD?

Are you comforted in knowing He will uphold you?

DAY 7
TOUGH LOVE IS GIVEN

A new commandment I give unto you, That ye love one another; as I have loved you, that ye also love one another.

JOHN 13:34 (KJV)

God is love. He sent His love to you while you were yet a sinner. His love is deeper and immeasurable in comparison to the love you have received beforehand. He loves you with a never changing love. Abounding in His love changes the posture of the love you give to others freely. God's love is a tough love that remains throughout all the seasons and the circumstances you be victorious. You will learn to love others as He continues to love you. You will no longer love others based on their reactions and actions to you. This is the evidence of God's love dwelling inside of you.

Dwelling in God's love teaches you how to separate your emotions that often enslave you to the freedom of loving with empathy. Removing judgement from your heart also refocuses you on the person and not sin. You learn to refocus on the person and not the sin. Jesus died on the cross and took the sins of all our sins. Don't forget that he also took the shame and guilt attached to each sin as well. We are a new, fresh canvas that He has covered in His love. It's not easy to love as God loves us. He loves us with a tough love. You will need daily to commit to surrender and abide with Him to reflect such a great love.

His is the only love that brings others to freedom and acceptance unconditionally. Keep your heart's posture in a place of gratitude knowing that you are loved with such a great love. The toughness in His love will grow and groom you into the righteousness He has called and fully equipped you to walk therein. Breathe in His sweet favor over your life as He softens those hardened areas of your heart that hold a scar from past hurts. A scar reflects and reminds you that you overcame what once hurt you but didn't destroy you. Great is His faithfulness! May His love flow through you.

God has given you the tools and the wisdom to sharpen the tools you use to maneuver and deal with those not like minded. Remember, you are called to love your enemies as you too were once in this place before you let the seed of His love take root in you. Loving others with God's love is tough as our flesh tries to revolt against through judgement wherein you have no place. God has chosen you to love others not in your strength but that of the Lord. Loving others is less about your relationship with them but about being a catalyst to guide them in embracing a relationship with God. Partner with your Heavenly Father asking him to place a guard upon your eyes, ears and tongue so that all will be in the unity of one love available to all through Jesus Christ.

7
TOUGH LOVE IS GIVEN

How do you see yourself loving others differently?

DAY 8

MISSION IN A DASH

> *To them who by patient continuance in well doing seek for glory and honour and immortality, eternal life:*

ROMANS 2:7 (KJV)

Part of God's faithfulness is His willingness to wait for your heart to line up with His. He is a good God. He goes before you and makes a way as well as continues to work behind the scenes for your good according to His purpose. As you walk in obedience and surrender, your faith will grow deeper. He will bring forth in due season a new thing.

God wants to partner with you into abundance. Choose this day going forward to lay down your life to Him. Posture your heart to seek Him first and ask, "What you can do for Him today?" He will not fail you! He will grow you into who He has called you to be, His child in whom He is well pleased. Contrary to popular belief, living the Christian life is not for the faint of heart. Your strength must be postured towards God with deep roots. His truth will be revealed when life's storm blows upon your safe banks. You will remain planted as strong tree bringing shelter to others. As you remain steadfast in running the good race of faith, press towards the good mark as your focus. God's Holy Word is one of instruction, truth and encouragement to carry us from glory to glory in all the seasons you journey through victoriously.

A tombstone reflects the time of birth and that of death. These are vitally important as they represent a life lived. However, it is the dash in between the dates that will reflect what was done with the life given. What are you doing with your dash? Go boldly! Love deeply! Daily clothe yourself with the armor of God and fight well the good battle as you stand on the battlefield of life. Forgive instantly and posture yourself to be a vessel that God permeates your life in both the good and bad in your life. Let your dash represent God in your life.

MISSION IN A DASH 8

How is His grace evidence through your kindness?

DAY 9
FIRST STEPS

So then faith cometh by hearing, and hearing by the word of God.

ROMANS 10:17 (KJV)

Stepping out of your comfort into God's unknown requires vision. Growing in God leads to trust in knowing His character as well as His unfailing love toward you. His will turn your shaky first steps of obedience into favor. Your faith will grow as your courage deepens to overcome fear. Take the first step! Seek out Jesus before worldly treasures. Seek His protection and tranquility in all you move toward. Let nothing of this world unsettle your heart as you keep a guard upon your heart. Be not discouraged through hurtful words or scars from your past. Simply call out to Jesus. He will restore and renew the inner you to wholeness.

Bring Him your weary heart and He will give you rest like none ever felt before. Rejoice that troubles are but a brief time. God is moving through your pain, revealing to you the disguise of blessings within the ache. Keep your perspective eternal. The Lord is positioning your steps for healing and breakthrough. Stand firm. Rest in grace upon grace. Partner with your heavenly Father today to embrace whatever this day may hold. Take His hand as you place your faith in Him.

He has already gone before you on this day to place provisions over you. Put on His mercies and grace given each day anew. God is using the pillar of fire to burn off your impurities as you move through life's test. He's writing your story, your testimony. But, God; is always followed by a semi colon reflecting more is to come. This is a divine picture of His faithfulness hand in hand with your mustard-seed faith, colliding to bring to light, through the pillar of the cloud, His plan of abundance over your life.

Partner with your Heavenly Father today to embrace whatever this day may hold. Take His hand as you place your faith in Him. He has already gone before you on this day to place provisions over you. Put on His mercies and grace given each day anew. God is using the pillar of fire to burn off your impurities as you move through life's test. He's writing your story, your testimony in due season. For such a time is this.

FIRST STEPS

What impact are your footsteps leaving behind?

SECTION 2

THE CATERPILLAR

Crawling Through Shattered Places

MATTHEW 5:6

As you continue to abide in Jesus Christ, a Divine grooming begins within you. Growth and change will take place starting on the inside working outward. The "old man" of sin is being shed from you as you begin to take on the "new man" of righteousness. You are growing confidently through prayer knowing that His plans are already in motion for your life. His eyes are upon you. He will grow your faith through your troubles leaving behind shattered strongholds. Your steps have been aligned from victory. You will be content as you journey from glory to glory. As you call upon the name of the Lord; he will be your refuge in all times of trials. He hears your deepest cries. God will go ahead of you to make a way where there seems to be no way. Despite the troubles that will come it is in them that you will see God's mercy and faithfulness over your comings and goings. He will shower you with peace beyond understanding. As you hold unto the promises of faith; the still small voice of the holy Spirit will empower you in moments of fear. Your rest awaits as you surrender your life and will to God's plan being renewed through restoration. What do you hunger and thirst for?

DAY 10
TRADING TROUBLES FOR PEACE

Now the Lord of peace himself give you peace always by all means. The Lord be with you all.

2 THESSALONIANS 3:16 (KJV)

Spending time with God more than a check mark on your daily to do list. You get to spend time with God. It is a privilege and honor to do so. You are valued and pursued by your creator. He delights in spending time with you. Surrender and be still as He sees your troubles. He knows that you are weary. God shows himself to you in the struggle. He is working on all things for your good. God is transforming you through the restoration of your mind, heart and soul. Put on the light yoke of Jesus and walk therein. Are you overwhelmed? Cast down the spirit of pride and come before God with humility.

Pride will quickly lead you astray down a crooked path. When you are weary draw near to Him. Reflect on His promise of yes and amen. The enemy uses the tool of discouragement to try to isolate you and place doubt and even fear to fog your vision. If you lack vision, then victory will not be attained. You are blessed and highly favored. Live a life being content and peace will remain in your life. Look to Jesus, the Prince of Peace when the schemes and lies of the enemy try to rattle you. Claim the Peace of Jesus over your life and all that's in it.

Don't open your door to chaos and confusion. He will give you rest as you remain a willing vessel that seeks God so to prevent spiritual bankruptcy. Humbly come with nothing in hand but a heart postured towards God. He will flourish your life in ways never imagined as you remain passionately serving Him with gratitude and joy. He will always meet you in your brokenness. He is not the God of one time, but he God of all time. He is the lifter of your head. Walk in His goodness and mercy as He promises them to follow you all of the days of your life.

Start each day intentionally with a grateful heart postured to God. Rejoice in the fresh canvas of a new day sealed in new mercy and grace. Invite the Holy spirit to walk through this day with you no matter what it may bring. Leave yesterday's offenses behind. Embrace kindness, compassion and God's love and plans for your day. As you splash these colors throughout your day on this clean canvas; remain humble. The masterpiece that you created comes from leaning into the Master and letting Him freely flow through you.

TRADING TROUBLES FOR PEACE

10

How has peace overcome fear in trials?

DAY 11
BE THE ONE

And one of them, when he saw that he was healed, turned back, and with a loud voice glorified God, And fell down on his face at his feet, giving him thanks: and he was a Samaritan.

LUKE 17:15-16 (KJV)

Throughout the hustle and bustle of your everyday life you most likely forget at least one thing daily. Luke 17 tells the story of ten men who had leprosy. They called out to Jesus, and he came to them and healed them. Yet, when one of the men realized that he was healed; he couldn't help to return to Jesus. He fell to his face with thanks before his healer, Jesus Christ. Ponder on that for a moment. Only one the often men came back, fell upon his face with thanks before his healer, Jesus Christ. Posture your heart to be the one who always comes with a grateful heart to offer gratitude first and needs second.

No matter the season or your place in it: thank God for his compassion and love towards you. Knowing exactly the posture of your heart; He sent His son, Jesus Christ so that you may walk in forgiveness throughout all the days of your life. Always be grateful for forgiveness first and God will add blessings beyond what you can store in your storehouse. Be the one who gives thanks. For clearer vision posture your heart toward God. Don't be alarmed should your worldly vision become a bit blurry but take note that your spiritual vision is clearer as your heart's desire is being revealed. The posture of your heart is the lens that corrects your vision. Just as wearing physical glasses improves your vision; the renewing of your mind brings restoration to your heart resulting in clearer vision as your eyes are fixed upon Him.

God will correct your spiritual vision when you intentionally lean into him. You will seek out opportunities to serve Him and others instead of gaining monetary riches. Challenge your self daily to be more like Jesus. Choose to be second and serve others first. Consider his ways through the decisions you make through godly wisdom. Be intentional as you follow in His purpose. Seek out all of God's given opportunities to serve others. Be ready and react in love instantly as you are being led by the Holy Spirit with directions on how to serve them. It is when your heart is postured to love and serve others with no strings attached that your heart is full and content. He is a good Father that withholds no blessings back from His children in whom He is well pleased. Living content may mean living outside of your comforts, but it is only then that God can truly bless you and bring you to contentment.

We are called to love one another as Christ has loved us. He gave us a promise that He would never leave us. He took this promise to the grave and continues to love us today. Jesus understands it truly takes the love of our Heavenly Father to love others. Love is not always an easy choice, but it is the necessary one needed. It's often the tough love that keeps us from being conformed to this world. Be committed to the labor of love God has placed within you. Look to Jesus to see the lengths God's love will reach to bring about change. Love is patient, be consistent to wait without grumbling and complaining. Draw upon the love of the Lord which is given from above to flow freely through you to give as it has been given to you. God's love will soften the hardest of hearts.

BE THE ONE

Will your heart be full of gratitude in sharing your story of restoration?

DAY 12

WORTH IT ALL

If a man therefore purge himself from these, he shall be a vessel unto honour, sanctified, and meet for the master's use, and prepared unto every good work. Flee also youthful lusts: but follow righteousness, faith, charity, peace with them that call on the Lord out of a pure heart.

2 TIMOTHY 2:21-22 (KJV)

Transformation comes as you commit your ways unto the Lord. Let go of your past and replace it with a Godly passion bearing the fruits of the spirit towards one another. Choose to live out a life of integrity and resist self-entitlement. May your character reflect that of God wrapped up in peace and love. Pay attention to every detail of every circumstance seeking God therein. Keep your mind free from the conformity of this world you journey through. Remember that you are in the world but not to be of it. You have been chosen by God with a purpose. You are called to be salt and light in the world. Humbly submit yourself unto the Lord through your afflictions. This season will strengthen you as you ponder upon the necessity of growth as you depend on delivery from despair to destiny.

Goodness and faithfulness are revealed in all seasons of your life. Take all your thoughts captive filtering them through the renewing of your mind by having the mind of Christ. You will have the strength and courage to move through whatever may come as you have the promise that God will bring you through. Leap in the joy of the Lord, Jesus Christ who will give you strength. Surround yourself with those God has divinely placed upon your path. What a blessing it is to know that when you are overwhelmed and weak that joy comes in the morning. Rest in his promises as you grow in fellowship with one another. Be confident in knowing that all the ebbs and flows of this life are truly worth it all.

What posture is your heart in? Are you in a teachable frame of mind? Who do you seek counsel? All these questions reflect your choices. Choose well! God has divinely placed purpose in your every step. Your heavenly Father is actively at work in every area of your life. Regardless of what may come, His grace is sufficient. He moves through your circumstances that challenge you to grow your faith. Daily surrender your will to God's will. Call upon the Holy Spirit to teach you so that your footsteps leave the print of Godly wisdom. Daily meditate upon god's word. His truth will transform your mind as you continue to spiritually mature. Come before His throne with a heart postured in gratitude. Lean upon His promises as you rest in knowing He is working all things for your good through Jesus Christ. Walk in the spirit therein lies the provision and promise of God.

Let your story be known. God whispers to you, "Come and sit with me." Do you hear Him? How will you respond? He will bring you to your knees first so that He can give you a firm foundation to stand firmly upon. As you daily choose to partner with Him, you will die more to self-gratification and grow more in His favor. He will lead you into unknown territory to sharpen your tools and deepen your faith for the times and seasons to come. You will travel through the wilderness but not be a resident of it. Your dependency of God will deepen as you find rest in His mercy and grace. Rejoice in his calling over your life. Shout your story from the mountaintops and speak it boldly as you walk through the valley. His story is your story of a love so pure none other can compare.

WORTH IT ALL

How did purging your desires align yourself to His blessings?

DAY 13
STEPPING INTO HIS CALLING

That if thou shalt confess with thy mouth the Lord Jesus, and shalt believe in thine heart that God hath raised him from the dead, thou shalt be saved.

ROMANS 10:9 (KJV)

Accept and believe that you were called and created in the goodness of God to be revealed. God's calling over your life will not be found within the circle of fear that encamps around you but in the realm of your Abba Father in Heaven. Change begins in the heart. The eighteen inches between your heart and mind is where your actions are formed. Once you, in obedience, surrender your life to God, fear must vacate as peace permeates every area of your life. God is not surprised that you are here; yet anticipates the journey that lies ahead for you. God's timing is perfect. He delights in you and gives you boldness to walk confidently in unknown territory. He is singing a new song of victory over you. He knows the battles you have overcome as He was there. He will apply His balm of healing to your battle scars. He hears your secret conversation and comforts you in it.

His love for you is unending. His favor will be over you as His promises unfold all around you. Boldly take your first step into the newness of your calling. You will continue to grow in good courage and bring others to clearly see the Glory of the Lord shining through you as you lead them into the arms of God. God holds in his hands the master key to unlock all your doors only chosen for you to walk through. These are doors to prosper you to live an abundant life in all areas of your life. It's not the position of your mind but your heart that God partners to open the door.

Build a good bridge for others to cross over from despair into hope. Confession is a posture of your heart that reflects surrender unto His ways and His will. Shaking off bad thoughts and habits requires a commitment to remain focused on bettering yourself. Your life will influence others either for good or bad, the choice is always yours to make. God has completely equipped you with the right tools and material needed to make a change in the rebuilding process called restoration. God will add unto all things that you do according to His will. Begin rebuilding your thought life today by building a bridge, tossing off the bad and letting His thoughts freely flow through you. As you build this bridge from your mind to your heart be sure to put up the railings of His love. Should you stumble, grab the railings and His love will stable you. The obedience of your thought life being renewed will be evident in your faith steps.

God's assurance of hope lives in; share it with the world. Greet everyone with a smile. Open the door for another. Show traveling mercies and let others in while in traffic to keep kindness flowing. You have no idea the things going on in another's life. However, you do know a God who loves them and will meet them wherever they are. Will you allow others to catch the living God shining through you by instant and random acts of kindness? You are making the world a better place just by the beauty you shower in simply being you and showing others their value is priceless. God's full assurance of hope lives in you just by who God created you to be.

STEPPING INTO HIS CALLING

Why are you fully confident to step into your calling?

DAY 14
THE LESS TRAVELED ROAD

> *Wherefore seeing we also are compassed about with so great a cloud of witnesses, let us lay aside every weight, and the sin doth so easily beset us, and let us run with patience the race that is set before us.*

HEBREWS 12:1 (KJV)

The journey of a thousand miles begins first the thought of the first step. When we choose to ask Jesus into our heart. The following steps are those of surrender unto God's will. Knowing not where we are going but being fully confident in knowing God has aligned your steps. . God has an unique plan over your life to bring into His purpose and calling over your life. No longer will your decisions be based on self-fulfillment but surrendered unto God for wisdom and discernment. You will walk by faith, not by sight.

You are no longer running this race alone. God has given you the Holy Spirit to equip you in the way that you should go. He will empower you as you are driven by His power as you lean into guidance and wisdom to get you to your new destination and keep you away from those who revolt against you. God's mercy and grace will cover you and keep you out of harm's way.

As you travel along; do not be alarmed by the sharp turns of unexpected events. You are never out of sight of your Heavenly Father. You will be fully equipped to choose wisely at the intersection of decisions and be confident that what may seem like a detour is meant to keep on the path less traveled. God knows all and sees all and because of His faithfulness you can rest and gain strength in knowing that he is leading you down the path for your good.

Rejoice in the confidence you have in trusting in His plans not yet fully revealed to you. As you continue to travel; lean into the truth you have gained through the meditation upon God's Word He is leading you into a breakthrough. He chose you to run this race at this time in this place. He will keep you focused on the journey even though you can't see what is on the horizon to come. That He is so near that He keeps your foot from slipping. He alone will make your crooked paths straight. You will not be set back by past thinking but advanced into victory from glory to glory.

14 THE LESS TRAVELED ROAD

How is this destination ahead like none other?

DAY 15
ABIDE MUCH?

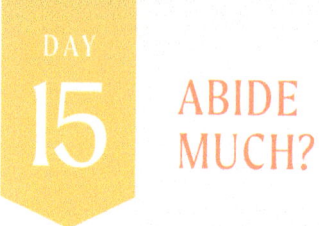

Call unto me, and I will answer thee, and show thee great and mighty things, which though knowest not.

JERMIAH 33:3 (KJV)

What will you do with God's mercy? Will you embrace it and lean into Him, or will you reject it and cling to your own understanding? God delights in mercy because of His great love toward us all. However, we all have free will and can choose not to accept His outreached hand of help. Stop the illusions of untruth about God's mercy in your heart and mind.

You have the mind of Christ and know that great is God's mercy toward all those who believe and walk in truth. Are you in despair? Ask God for mercy. He hears you and will cast your iniquities into the depths of the sea. His mercy brings freedom.

Now you walk upright in His truth because of His compassion. Shower others with His mercy as you lend a hand to help another out of a pit of despair. Guide them in His truth as they are set free and walk out God's mercy. Your adversary, the devil tries to use the distractions of life and the whispers of doubt to discourage you in your journey. God's promises give you unlimited resources to overcome deceitful schemes and lies against God's plan over your life.

Your life is being groomed as you abide in the vine, Jesus Christ. God attends to your life like that of a great gardener. He sees the evidence of the seed that is still not evident to others clearly. He does the divine pruning in your life removing those branches not bringing forth good fruit. There is healing in the pain pruning brings. Good fruit will spring forth as the Holy Spirit indwells within and heals you from the inside out. You will be stretched beyond your furthest imaginations. God will bring forth a new thing in through this season of abiding. Rejoice in the great and mighty things God has and will continue to do in you.

15 ABIDE MUCH?

What great and mighty things has He shown you?

DAY 16: REFLECT AND RESPOND

Remember ye not the former things, neither consider the things of old. Behold, I will do a new thing: how it shall spring forth; shall ye not know it? I will even make a way in the wilderness, and rivers in the desert.

ISAIAH 43:18-19 (KJV)

New each morning, God writes afresh the pages of your life story. He brings to life words of His unfailing purpose. His great mercy and grace are evident in your everlasting hope through Jesus Christ. Be still as you meditate upon His faithfulness. Look at where He has brought you from in the past, only to plunge into the new thing He alone is bringing forth for you. Receive and shower others with all He has given to you. He is near and He sees you. Answer His call when He calls to you. Broken, hopeless, heavy burdened—just come as you are. He is the lifter of your head. Shake off those grave clothes and take on the light yoke of Jesus. Stand straight and rejoice! Quickly tell others what you know. He alone has straightened you and the path to His purpose over your life. Hallelujah!

When the winds of crisis come, be still in your spirit. Let God rise you up as you soar with hope above treacherous winds. Hope is an active, complete picture God is always applying to your day. Your hope is the passion you must seek a pathway when there seems no clear way.

You are never alone. Trying times bring twisted lies that can lead you into feeling isolated. Jesus is nearest to the brokenhearted. When you find the day challenging and you are bent in despair, calm yourself and call out to Jesus When the winds of crisis come, be still in your spirit. Let God rise you up as you soar with hope above treacherous winds. Hope is an active, complete picture God is always applying to your day.

Through life you will soar through all it brings in His hope. Hope changes you. Life is better because you have chosen not to be bitter but better because of all life brings you. Soar in His hope! He is near and He sees you. Answer His call when He calls to you. Broken, hopeless, heavy burdened—just come as you are. He is the lifter of your head. Shake off those grave clothes and take on the light yoke of Jesus. Stand straight and rejoice! Quickly tell others what you know. He alone has straightened you and the path to His purpose over your life. Hallelujah!

When the winds of crisis come, be still in your spirit. Let God rise you up as you soar with hope above treacherous winds. Hope is an active, complete picture God is always applying to your day. Your hope is the passion you must seek a pathway when there seems no clear way.

REFLECT AND RESPOND?

What is the new thing springing forth in you?

DAY 17
A WELL CONVERSATION

Jesus said unto her, Go, call thy husband, and come hither. The woman answered and said, I have no husband. Jesus said unto her, Thou hast well said, I have no husband; For thou hast had five husbands; and he whom thou now hast is not thy husband: in that saidst thou truly.

JOHN 4:16-18 (KJV)

Jesus and His disciples went through Samaria on their way to Galilee. Once they arrived, the disciples went to town to get food as Jesus stayed behind. He waited patiently in the heat of the day for a Samaritan woman to come draw from the well. She traveled alone and in the heat of the day because she was a social outcast. She was known for being married five times.

Upon arriving at the well, Jesus immediately began to break down social barriers by asking her for a drink of water. He listened intently as she harshly reminded Him that there is no association between a Jew and a Samaritan. She then added, "And you have no vessel to draw your water and the well is deep."

It was at that moment Jesus revealed His purpose for being at the well. He explained the water she is drawing is temporary for physical thirst. He offered to quench her spiritual thirst, explaining that whoever drinks this water of salvation will become a fountain of water springing up into everlasting life. In awe and acknowledgment of who was offering her a drink, she accepted it. Quickly she ran to tell the others in town, leaving her vessel at the well as her thirst had been quenched with everlasting life.

The love of Christ can't flow through you when you have an undercurrent of strife. Strife will rob you of the harmony and peace God desires for you to live in. You can embrace the unity of the spirit and the bond of peace as the love of Christ flows through you. Humility, gentleness, patience, and love are four words that reflect each other.

A WELL CONVERSATION 17

What truths did God reveal to you that none other knew?

DAY 18
PROPER LENS BRINGS PROPER PERSPACTIVE

That ye put off concerning the former conversation the old man which is corrupt according to the deceitful lusts: And be renewed in the spirit of your mind; And that ye put on the new man, Which after God is created in righteousness and true holiness.

EPHESIANS 4:22-24 (KJV)

Jesus tells us that in the world we will have trials and tribulations. Remain in a posture of expectancy for this to happen. We are not to be downcast for we have a perpetual hope in knowing that He has overcome the world. All things are being worked for our good according to His plan. His thoughts and ways are higher than ours. Leaning into Jesus puts you in the correct posture to renew your mind to put knowledge turned into wisdom into motion.

Check your attitude when trials knock on your door. Be wise to not answer every knock upon your door. Chaos and confusion are tools of the enemy trying to steal your vision, bringing forth doubt and fear. Remain humble and fear will disperse as you rejoice in the Lord. Choose to look past the negative through the lens of hope, His divine perspective.

God is singing a new song of redemption over you. Do you hear Him? Lean into His sweet harmony over your life. Rejoice in His harmony by keeping your spirit humble and being ready to give an answer for the hope that you have. Remain true to seeking out His plans over your day. Start each day with a humble spirit and a heart postured in gratitude.

Only God will turn your past for His Glory. He will turn your messes into messages to teach others valuable lessons. Lessons that will shake off the old man and welcome in the new man through Divine direction. Inhale hope and exhale despair as you refocus hearing His voice speaking His truth to every circumstance.

18
PROPER LENS BRINGS PROPER PERSPECTIVE

How was your vision made clear?

SECTION 3

THE CHRYSALIS
Waiting and Cultivating Resilience

HEBREWS 6:19

Choosing to die to self is a choice of free will. It is deciding to willingly go through an adverse experience and retreat within. Come in, away from the noise and chaos of this world. Seek out the gentle and calm spirit that awaits to embrace you due to the changes you've grown through. God has brought you here in perfect timing. Breathe in peace and exhale all other fear. Ponder on the journey thus far. What an amazing transformation has already happened within you. You are surrounded by His promises and provisions. You are here because your heart is postured in gratitude. It is well in your soul. No longer will you be recognized the same way. Those who know you best will see a difference that no words can fully capture. His everlasting compassion and love have changed you through resilience. What will you surrender cultivate in your life?

DAY 19
SPIRITUAL REBOUND

The Lord shall preserve thee from all evil: he shall preserve thy soul. The Lord shall preserve thy going out and thy coming in from this time forth, and even for evermore.

PSALM 121:7-8 (KJV)

Are you praying for a breakthrough? Rest in peace as you abound in hope know God is your rock and high tower of refuge. May you draw upon His truths. God's love is unconditional, and His promises are infallible. The good things He has called into your life are unstoppable. Call upon God in good seasons and those of despair. Just as Joshua trusted in God to make him victorious in the battle in Jericho; God will make the walls of despair to fall around you.

Other times He doesn't allow the move the mountain in front of you to be moved. Take heed and find comfort. Don't sit in defeat; but rejoice as you rise and face the mountain before you. Keep your eyes fixed on His unfailing plan already in motion. Whispers of defeat will be heard when your eyes are focused on the limitations of the walls you built that God never intended to hold you. He will establish your footsteps to climb the mountain and keep you from all harm. He is so near that He will not even allow your foot to slip. You may feel that you are dealing with loss upon loss, but you are being carried through grace upon grace.

Learning to embrace whatever each day may bring is done through maturity and surrender. Choosing to partner with Jesus and walk justly will keep you from being led by your heart or feelings. Confession makes your bond with God stronger and brings you to a place of a new and Christ centered attitude. Walk humbly knowing that God sees, hears and knows all things both spoken and thought. Remain positive and know that God is working all things for your good.

Change is a necessary for growth. Seeking wisdom has many layers. The first layer is humility. This requires you to surrender in asking God for help because you don't know the answers. The second layer is wisdom. Knowledge is gained when you remain in a teachable posture, but God turns it into wisdom when you remain always intentional in seeking God's truth. Thirdly, choose to be like minded so therefore you will reap in the blessings of God.

SPIRITUAL REBOUND

10

How has the Lord preserved you in your going out and coming in?

DAY 20
PURE AND PEACEABLE

And be not conformed to this world: but be ye transformed by the renewing of your mind, that ye may prove what is that good, and acceptable, and perfect will of God.

ROMANS 12:2 (KJV)

God has called you to live out a pure and peaceable life. Choosing to make a change in your life will begin with the inward renewal of your mind. As you grow daily your inner spirit is transformed into the likeness of Jesus, from glory to glory. The new man coming forth will reflect new values with integrity in the development of new character. You will be renewed by The Holy Spirit as he continues to guide you through all your comings and goings. As you surrender your life to God, by His will, He changes the impossible to possible. He reveals the gift He has placed in you as you posture your heart to serve others with love and compassion. The presence of Jesus Christ in your life leads you to walk in the way God has called. You will apply

His wisdom in all your words and deeds. A perimeter of peace will surround you as you continually seek to walk by faith and not by sight. Your victorious steps have been ordered by God. His mercies and grace are new each day.

Remain steadfast and confident when challenges arise. Remember, and cling to, the promises He has spoken over your life. The weapon may be formed against you, but God promises that it will not prosper. Resist the temptations that try to entangle you, staying focused on the things of God. That which is pure, honest, true, lovely and of good report keep you rooted deeply in good soil bearing good fruit in due season. Surrendering all thoughts and actions to God's will. God has given favor to move into the core of His design in your life. His fullness of favor is how God reaches those around you as He brings you into the fullness of His covenant over you. He chose you because you submitted yourself as a willing vessel. He can work through all the seasons of your life. Obedience to God's calling isn't always easy but always brings glory to God and direction and correction to others through words of encouragement and guidance. You are in the perfect will of God as you walk in the inheritance He has for you.

20
PURE AND PEACEABLE

Are your works of faith evident in your words and deeds?

DAY 21: YIELD TO WISDOM AND PEACE

But the wisdom that is from above is first pure, then peaceable, gentle, and easy to be intreated, full of mercy and good fruits, without partiality, and without hypocrisy.

JAMES 3:17 (KJV)

God has chosen you to be part of a community reflecting His peace. Be careful and take captive all your thoughts with His righteousness before they form words and are spoken through raw emotions. Pass all your words through the filter of peace. Be intentional to use your words to build others up. Meet others in their brokenness and remain present throughout their rebuilding process. Unity is the core to maintaining peace with others. It takes a community (village) to grow in a safe and loving environment.

Growing up spiritually in a community of fellow believers is essential to your growth. As you lean on and learn from those who have been where you are going; it will encourage you to do so in due season. Walk in humility as you share each other's stories to bond as you grow together. Yielding to wisdom will also deepen your ability to move through a trial as you guard your heart against temptations that come against pure peace from above.

God wants to move you through doubt and those things that tempt you keeping you in a victim mind set. Be confident and unwavering as you claim God's promise that" No weapon formed against you shall prosper. The weapon will be formed, but God promises that no harm will come to you. Remember who you are and to whom you belong. You are a mighty child of God. The winds may blow, and the floods may rise but you are kept by the hand of God. You will not be overcome, and your light will not go out. Allow your light of peace to shine brilliantly and burn off the fog that may hinder your clearer vision.

God grows you through tests and trials to develop your character according to His plan. He will put you through the refiner's fire to burn off the impurities of the world. When you prioritize God, His goodness surrounds you. When you are showered by pain, find refuge under

God's promise that covers you like an umbrella. Pray with expectancy when the unexpected happens. Seek wisdom through His Word to be on guard from the fiery darts of defeat and despair that may fly your way. Stay connected to those who encourage you as you grow into His plans to prosper you.

YIELD TO WISDOM AND PEACE 21

What does this bear in your life?

DAY 22
A WORK OF WORSHIP

With good will doing service as to the Lord, and not to men.

EPHESIANS 6:7 (KJV)

Tunnel vision is when all you can focus on is what is in front of you. When the sides feel restrictive, pray more passionately. Encourage yourself by speaking God's truths over your doubts. Flex your faith muscle. Trust and believe in your journey. Don't be downcast but be of good cheer. Pursue His righteousness. Seek His purpose that brings fulfillment into your life. Posture your heart to sow seeds of kindness as you do all deeds in His strength.

He hears your prayers and will deliver you from your troubles. No matter how long or dark the tunnel may appear, His light at the end of it will guide you through. Tunnel vision, although challenging, will reveal where your hope comes from as you truly see His faithfulness toward you. You never walk alone. You are called to this place for His Glory.

You are a missionary right where you are. God uses all of your work and efforts along the way to bring you to a place of newness. The work God is doing through you in not necessarily rewarded through an earthly paycheck but is making Heavenly treasures. God is molding and shaping the gifts in you according to His purpose to shine hope in a world where darkness seems more present. But God is ever present always.

As you posture your heart to service your blurred vision becomes clearer to His purpose. You are fully equipped to do all that He has called you to do for His Kingdom. You are chosen to do all things with excellence unto the Lord. Your attitude and dedication will set you apart from others you may work with. Be encouraged that you may be an encouragement for them to strive to be better instead of being bitter by going the extra mile. Work is designed to bring personal fulfillment. Choose to turn your fulfillment into worship as you do it all unto Him.

22
A WORK OF WORSHIP

How has your life changed to honor God?

DAY 23
WINGS AND ROOTS

But they that wait upon the LORD shall renew their strength; they shall mount up with wings as eagles; they shall run, and not be weary; and they shall walk, and not faint.

ISAIAH 40:31 (KJV)

Remain saturated in the Word of God. When your adversary, the devil, seeks to make you doubt and stumble, you will remain steadfast. Be sober as you remain aware of his schemes and lies to try to bring division and fear. Keep your focus on God's promises and favor over your days. Surrender not to fear but delight in testing, knowing it is adding to your testimony. Daily shake off old grave clothes and purposefully dress in the armory of God. Guard your heart as you step into each day. This too shall pass.

God is using even this for your good. He has aligned your steps starting in victory. Rejoice in knowing that it is through the fiery darts that you become established in your faith, strengthened through who goes before you and settled in knowing who fights for you and sings a new song over you. This is the place you have fought to arrive at. Be still and in His time, He will turn your suffering to abundance of perfection. Rejoice and remain steadfast.

God has created you for relationships. He knows the value in them and even gave us an order to keep them in priority. Friendship is a gift from the above. Nothing grows you like a friendship. Nothing compares to the depth of knowledge friendship brings to our table. A friend reflects a commitment, some deeper than others. It is sown together with the golden thread of love through God. Friendship is one of many masterpieces God designs. We are better and reflect a better side of ourselves as others reveal it and gives you wings to soar as you are called to do.

We share our deepest secrets only with our most treasured friends. God shows you through the seasons of your life who your closest friends are. The ones who do the "just because" are the ones who treasure you in their life. They reach out at the right time, they speak the right word, and they are your place of refuge. They choose to learn when to give you wings or roots. Friends are there for one another, through good seasons and bad. It does take time to let others in your deep place, but it's worth the time and journey.

23
WINGS AND ROOTS

How has God given you both roots and wings?

DAY 24
ANCHOR OF HOPE

Which hope we have as an anchor of the soul both sure and stedfast, and which entereth into that within the veil;

HEBREWS 6:19 (KJV)

Hopelessness is a shared feeling. You may feel as though you have hit rock bottom, and all hope is gone. Hope is not a feeling it is a truth and promise of God. Find comfort in knowing that God is your rock you can find comfort in life shaking times. You are not on sinking sand. You are not alone. You are being held under His wing of protection. Fear can't touch you as you are covered by His spirit of peace.

God is faithful to move with you through all your seasons of discouragement and difficulties. He will turn your crooked road of suffering into a straight path to help others found in your same position as you are strengthened for His Glory. Your faith grows through adversity and new life is brought forth.

Restoration comes from brokenness and suffering. You have found His favor remains anchored in His hope.

God is closest to you in your brokenness. Choose to become an open vessel where He will bring you up out of the pit with divine purpose and understanding. He will place your feet on new ground. Your purpose is to be renewed in your mind, heart and soul. Transformation happens when you are open to God moving through you and using your life as a venue for others to be encouraged in His faithfulness through His goodness.

24 ANCHOR OF HOPE

How has hope anchored you in safety?

DAY 25
ENDURE THE WAITING AND EMBRACE THE BLESSINGS

But watch thou in all things, endure afflictions, do the work of an evangelist, make full proof of thy ministry.

2 TIMOTHY 4:5 (KJV)

While you are waiting, be busy working and seeking God's will. Endure the suffering you face without murmuring or complaining by seeking God's instructions through it. Think about the lessons we learn from the book of Job. God allowed Job to be tested because He knew the posture of Job's heart. Job endured the suffering and reaped twice the blessing of his loss. Believe in God's provision and plan over your life.

Believe in yourself as you step into this new season. Trust God has placed "your people" in your life to speak truth into you. Remain humble and steadfast, all the time growing in your knowledge and wisdom. Have eyes to see and receive what God has already spoken into motion. Get to stepping. You've endured the suffering, embrace the blessings. God will create in you a divine balance between waiting and blessings. It is in this place of surrender and submission that you can hear God clearly. Doing the outward from what God is springing forth in your life brings harmony with God.

It is God's desire for you to live a peaceable life as much as possible. As you walk in the newness of His likeness; you will be drawn to those who harmoniously beside you. Harmony removes the uncomfortable connection and makes family out of who were once people passing in your life. It is in the time of waiting that God really grows the connection and grows you in the stillness of hearing others journey. You have a spirit of peace that freely flows from one to another. It is also in this season of waiting that often your direction shifts, or the best made plans change direction. God uses every moment, person and situation to completely grow you into being well rounded to be groomed for excellence.

Be mindful of the choices you make with your free will. Capture the opportunities that lie before you with joy. Always keep God your priority. Choose to renew your strength daily by leaning into the Holy Spirit as you are guided throughout your day. Cling to the promises of God that give you hope to embrace and endure seasons of adversity that you may encounter. Meditate daily on God's Word so you will be in good posture to answer whatever comes your way. God will remain near and always hear your cries, prayers and praise. It is in due season the harvest will come, but for now you must rest well in the waiting.

24

**ENDURE THE WAITING AND
EMBRACE THE BLESSING**

How did waiting bless you?

SECTION 4

THE BUTTERFLY
Blessed Flight of Hope

JEREMIAH 17:7

Openly receiving what God has called you into is a blessing beyond measure. As you release your control to God your metamorphosis continues in His presence. It is when you can release your demands and be consumed by His provision of what is needed so that you will truly be weightless. Embrace the new you that has sprung forth from a place no longer seen where a seed of hope was present and taken in. Rest and be renewed in the lightness of hope. This moment has been in motion since before the time that you were knitted together in your mother's womb. Awaken to the new life that God has promised to them who love Him and surrender their life to Him. You have been chosen for His divine transformation. The renewal of your heart is postured in gratitude. You are exactly where you are called to be as you prepare to take flight. Spread your wings and take flight as the gentle breeze of hope lifts you higher and higher for His Glory.

DAY 26
BREATH OF HOPE

But unto every one of us is given grace according to the measure of the gift of Christ.

EPHESIANS 4:7 (KJV)

Take a deep breath in, and now exhale slowly. God has called us to give unto others as He has given unto us. God gives abundantly. He forgives you immediately, and you are to do the same to others. As you gaze upon this canvas of a day, choose wisely the colors you splash not only on your own canvas but also on the canvases of others by your words and deeds. Splash the bright colors of hope, peace, and joy over any darkened areas.

May the color of forgiveness wrapped up in God's love bring forth God's masterpiece revealed on each canvas. Lighten another's load by exhaling forgiveness as it has been given unto you, immediate and without reminder of your shortcomings. Breathe in hope! Walking in forgiveness keeps your load light as you lay down the burden of offense and walk in His promises.

God's mercies are grace are afresh each morning. Allow them to freely flow through the pages of your life story. He brings to life words of His unfailing love towards you. His great mercy and grace are evident in your everlasting hope through Jesus Christ. Ponder and meditate upon His great faithfulness.

Take a moment of reflection of where He has led and what He has brought you through. He is bringing you into a new thing. Are you seeking Him for the newness within you? Share your story. Tell of His great mercies over your life. The moments where His grace changed your story. Embrace the winds of crisis when they blow all around you. Surrender to His plan and He will be with you. He will either calm the wind or you, His child. You are not alone. Your hope will pave a path to clear your way for clearer vision. Soar above it all on the wings of His love.

26

BREATH OF HOPE

How has hope breathed into your new life?

DAY 27
ORDAINED IN LOVE

> *Ye have not chosen me, but I have chosen you, and ordained you, that ye should go and bring forth fruit, and that your fruit should remain: that whatsoever ye shall ask of the Father in my name, he may give it you. These things I command you, that ye love one another.*

JOHN 15:16-17 (KJV)

Did you know that each one of God's children are ordained? You are ordained, brought into godly order, to love others as He loves you with a never-ending love. His love does not come with conditions but is given freely. Love is a choice followed by demonstration. He is your first love. Remember to always keep first things first, and as His plan will flourish in your life. We can only truly love others with God's love. Sow seeds of hope, mercy, joy, forgiveness, and grace into soils enriched in His love. May this fruit bring a sweet fragrance unto the Heavens above.

Remain certain in what and whom you believe in. Is it well with your soul? Will you choose to dig in your heels as you study and meditate upon His word daily? God is certain; meaning that He is precise, clear and always in perfect time. Are your eyes focused on Him who is faithful in all His ways. You may not always understand His certainty, but you will see His provision in due time if you faint not. Selah means to rest and reflect on the prior information. You are loved with great love. God speaks clearly, not in chaos or riddles.

He speaks firmly in words of hope and direction to guide you through uncertainties so that you will not stumble, but rest in places of hope and security. His purpose surrounds you with provision according to His plan. His peace will have perfect aim in your life. Choose to grow in a community where others are growing alongside you. God created you for relationships to grow among like minded people. Iron sharpens iron. You are needed.

Serve one another in humility. Choose to be second and serve others and your needs will be met. God delights in unity throughout His people. Remember to always keep first things first, and as His plan will flourish in your life. We can only truly love others with God's love. Sow seeds of hope, mercy, joy, forgiveness, and grace into soils enriched in His love. May this fruit bring a sweet fragrance unto the Heavens above.

Don't conform to the ways of this world but be salt and a beacon of light to all those you cross paths with. Season other's life with the kindness and share the promises of God even in the moments of brokenness. Come as you are. Rejoice in knowing that he is the lifter of your head. Be a good student and always be ready to give an answer to your life story and how God has ordained you in love.

ORDAINED IN LOVE

How has His love transformed you to bear fruit?

DAY 28
LIVING OUT A LIFE OF EXCELLENCE

But God, who is rich in mercy, for His great love wherewith He loved us, even when we were dead in sins hath quickened us together with Christ, (by grace ye are saved;)

EPHESIANS 2:4-5 (KJV)

Lost vision reflects forfeited hope. When your vision has been temporarily shifted from God your vision becomes foggy. Let these words clear the fog for you to see clearly. God has placed more within you than you could ever be aware of as it is not always within your sight. However, it is always within God's vision. God's ways are above ours. Don't settle for the life you are living out every day. Dig deeper! Set yourself for excellence. Choose to be a partner with God in prayer as your run out your Christian race with great endurance and patience.

Be intentional to align yourself and your day with God's will and plan. Be conscious to reflect and ponder throughout the day being aware of God's will and plan. His provision and presence encamp around you. Choose to partner with God before the door of opportunity is before you. As He has aligned your steps to this place at this time you must choose to step towards it. As you step in faith and walk towards the door; turn the doorknob in confidence to step into your next season of promise and accomplishments. Growth awaits you. Restored joy, peace and hope will overflow where you once were overcome. God delights in your obedience. Come and choose to live out a life of excellence according to His purpose to which you are called.

God has chosen you to be His child, who He has fully equipped to fulfill His plan to live out an abundant life. Be encouraged when trials come; as you are called to be more than a conqueror; you are an overcomer. God shows his favor, guidance and provision. He keeps His word because he is truth. No matter where your road leads, you are not there alone. God even grows you through the time where you felt isolate in an abandoned land. He fights for you. You will learn to lean more into God as time carries on. Only God can bring forth a new thing in barren and parched areas. Surrender your unbelief. He is doing a new thing in you. Receive it, believe in it and walk in it with boldness and confidence as He closed the wrong doors in your life.

Part of God's faithfulness is His willingness to wait for your heart to line up with His. He goes before you to make a way as well as continuing to work through you. As you walk in obedience and surrender; your faith will grow deeper. He will bring forth in due season a new thing. God wants to partner with you in abundance. Choose this day going forward to lay down your life to Him. Posture your heart to seek Him first and humbly ask what can you do for Him today? He will not fail you. He will grow you into who He has called you to be, His child in whom He is well pleased.

28 LIVING OUT A LIFE OF EXCELLENCE

What is your story of grace?

DAY 29: DWELL AND BE TRANSFORMED

> *If ye then be risen with Christ, seek those things which are above, where Christ sitteth on the right hand of God. Set your affection on things above, not on things on the earth.*

COLOSSIANS 3:1-2 (KJV)

Not all your habits are even consciously made. Truth be known, we all have habits we don't know why we have, or when they started. God has chosen you. He's called you to be kingdom minded. Be on guard not to fall into the pit of comparison that leads you down the prideful road of unhealthy competition, compelling you toward fast-fading self-promotion. God is your promoter. Healthy competition builds one another up, leaving no one on the sidelines. As you develop and grow in godly habits, His guidance will lead you from grace to grace as you give God all the glory due unto Him.

Meet with God throughout your day. Meditate upon His Word. Seek His leading over your ways. He will reveal the hidden treasures for His children. They are above this world, free from the moths and rust of the world we walk in daily. Fix your eyes upon them as you daily posture your heart toward Your heavenly Father. Speak to Him in a way others can't hear through the language of prayer.

Be mindful to pray for others aloud as you bring them before His throne of mercy and grace. Ask God to help you remove unhealthy habits and replace them with wholesome habits that will give Him glory as you walk with confidence and boldness in the abundant life, He has called you to live out. God is omnipresent. He is your safe refuge. Wherever you are the winds of change will blow. What was once a desolate location God is bring forth much fruit and abundance into your growth. Now you find yourself leaving your place of comfort and being stretched to grow into newness. As you stand at the crossroads you and cry out to the Holy Spirit to help you; you feel His presence and know this time like all others you will be in good hands. He will make the right way for you. Be prepared and in expectancy as trials will come and with them comes growth. Trials have gotten you right here at this very moment. God sees and knows the way, as He is your way maker. His love is not defined in the trials but is seen in the way He brought you through the trial. His love for you is constant and everlasting. You are His beloved and he delights in you.

DWELL AND BE TRANSFORMED 29

Where did transformation begin in your life?

DAY 30
FAVOR AS YOU ABIDE IN REST

For thus saith the Lord God, the Holy One of Israel; In returning and rest shall ye be saved; in quietness and in confidence shall be your strength: and ye would not.

ISAIAH 30:15 (KJV)

God created you with great interest and intention with uniqueness like none other. He has placed gifts for your calling and wisdom to apply the knowledge you are gaining. Growing in Jesus means to be abiding your life in him especially when you are resting. Run the race daily but posture for a place of daily reflection where it will be well with your soul. Peace and perfect love are the fruits of abiding with Jesus. God has placed boundaries in place from the beginning to guard quietness and confidence. Rest is a boundary needed to resist spiritual chaos and confusion.

Even before you were formed in your mother's womb, God knew you. Pause for a moment and let that settle in you. He knows who you are today, and He knows all about your yesterdays. He alone knows what tomorrow holds for you. You are His amazing, wonderfully made creation. He delights in being a part of your growing through every milestone. He lovingly and purposefully places you where you have been and leads the way to where you're going.

Delight daily in His ways. Be faithful in living your life out loud as you share your testimony with those brought upon your path. May the vibrant colors of His love, mercy, and grace outshine the trials that God has carried you through. It is God's grace upon grace that shines as a beacon of hope through you that draws others. Great is His faithfulness. His favor is a banner over your life as you remain available, humble, and obedient.

May your words be sweet as honey. Walk in love and pray more as you choose to complain less. Choose this day and every day as a platform to be grateful. Be mindful of the choices you make with free will. Capture the opportunities that lie before you with joy. Delight yourself in the Lord. He has equipped you with all that you need to press through the struggle. Struggles remove the unnecessary and replace it with the sufficient. Remain steadfast. Keep your head lifted and your eyes focus on His will. He knows you and knows who you are becoming.

FAVOR AS YOU ABIDE IN REST 30

What strength did you gain in resting in Him?

DAY 31
WHAT IS YOUR LIFE BUILDING?

But so shall it be among you: but whosoever will be great among you, shall be your minister: And whosoever of you will be the chiefest, shall be servant of all. For even the Son of man came not to be ministered unto, but to minister, and to give his life a ransom for many.

MARK 10:43-45 (KJV)

Challenge yourself every day to be like Jesus as you posture your heart to be second and to serve others first. Consider your ways through the decisions you make filtered by Godly wisdom. Be intentional as you follow in His purpose. Seek out all of God's given opportunities to serve others. Be ready and react in love instantly as you are being led by the Holy Spirit with directions on how to serve others.

It is when your heart is postured to love and serve others that your heart is full and content. He is a good Father who holds no blessings back from His children in whom He is well pleased. Living content may mean living outside of your comforts, but it is only then that God can truly bless you and bring you to contentment.

Love others with empathy. Empathy moves you from self freely choosing to be second and come alongside another to give them hope and support. Choosing to bend down and lift the burden of another shows the supreme love that deeply dwells within you from God. Lean into God's love to give others strength. Focus on how you can pray and invite the Holy spirit to intervene. Loving fervently moves you from a posture of vengeance to one of sweet victory. Choose to love others intentionally and sincerely.

Start your day with thanksgiving unto God. Rejoice in the fresh canvas of a new day. Invite the Holy Spirit to walk with you through whatever this day holds. Leave yesterday's offenses behind. Embrace kindness, compassion, and God's love. As you splash these colors on this clean canvas of a day, remain humble. The masterpiece you created comes from leaning into the Master and Him flowing through you. Now spread your wings fearlessly as you soar into your journey of hope. May the beautiful colors of His design shine brilliantly leading others into restoration. Tell your story leading others to God who is full of new beginnings.

WHAT IS YOUR LIFE BUILDING 31

Will you be an open vessel for God to move through and minister to others?

In Dedication

I dedicate this book to God first who has been faithful to show me His calling during my brokenness. His favor has given me wings to soar in hope.

I dedicate this book to my wonderful sons, Chris and Josh. Thank you for all the wonderful adventures we have shared that have broadened my horizons. Your love has always given me the courage to become more than I could ever imagine. My favorites stories will always be first and foremost the ones we shared together.

I dedicate this book to all of you who have sowed seeds of hope in my life. Your words of encouragement have helped me press on through the fear of taking the first steps into new, unknown territory.

Lastly, to my publisher Tim Twigg and all those at Arrow Press publishing who took these raw devotions from a place of brokenness and put life in them. Your dedication has championed me to give tools of encouragement to others to embrace change through hope and restoration.

www.ingramcontent.com/pod-product-compliance
Lightning Source LLC
Chambersburg PA
CBHW061809070526
44586CB00024B/2770